SO-BBC-218

A NOTE TO PARENTS

When your children are ready to "step into reading," giving them the right books—and lots of them—is as crucial as giving them the right food to eat. **Step into Reading Books** present exciting stories and information reinforced with lively, colorful illustrations that make learning to read fun, satisfying, and worthwhile. They are priced so that acquiring an entire library of them is affordable. And they are beginning readers with an important difference—they're written on four levels.

Step 1 Books, with their very large type and extremely simple vocabulary, have been created for the very youngest readers. **Step 2 Books** are both longer and slightly more difficult. **Step 3 Books,** written to mid-second-grade reading levels, are for the child who has acquired even greater reading skills. **Step 4 Books** offer exciting nonfiction for the increasingly proficient reader.

Children develop at different ages. **Step into Reading Books,** with their four levels of reading, are designed to help children become good—and interested—readers *faster*. The grade levels assigned to the four steps—preschool through grade 1 for Step 1, grades 1 through 3 for Step 2, grades 2 and 3 for Step 3, and grades 2 through 4 for Step 4—are intended only as guides. Some children move through all four steps very rapidly; others climb the steps over a period of several years. These books will help your child "step into reading" in style!

Text copyright © 1989 by Stephen Krensky. Illustrations copyright © 1989 by James Watling. All rights reserved under International and Pan-American Copyright Conventions. Published in the United States by Random House, Inc., New York, and simultaneously in Canada by Random House of Canada Limited, Toronto.

Library of Congress Cataloging-in-Publication Data:
Krensky, Stephen. Witch hunt: It happened in Salem Village. (Step into reading. A Step 4 book) SUMMARY: An account of the madness that overtook Salem Village, Massachusetts, when several young girls accused a number of adults in the community of being witches.
1. Witchcraft—Massachusetts—Salem—Juvenile literature. 2. Salem (Mass.)—Social life and customs—Juvenile literature. [1. Witchcraft—Massachusetts-Salem. 2. Salem (Mass.)—History—Colonial period, ca. 1600–1775] I. Watling, James, ill. II. Title. III. Series BF1576.K74 1989 974.4′502 88-42865 ISBN: 0-394-81923-3 (pbk.); 0-394-91923-8 (lib. bdg.)

Manufactured in the United States of America 1 2 3 4 5 6 7 9 0

STEP INTO READING is a trademark of Random House, Inc.

Step into Reading

WITCH HUNT

It Happened in Salem Village

By Stephen Krensky
Illustrated by James Watling

A Step 4 Book

Random House New York

51052

1

The Madness Begins

The winter of 1692 started out like any other winter in Salem Village, Massachusetts. It was cold and it was dark. The roads were often covered by deep drifts of snow.

Visitors were rare, but those passing through could always warm themselves at the parsonage. Samuel Parris, the minister of the village church, lived there with his wife Elizabeth, his daughter Betty, his niece Abigail, and two slaves, John and Tituba.

It was the minister's duty to take care of people. Every Sunday, Mr. Parris preached in church for two or three hours. The villagers, he warned, must be constantly on guard. The devil and his tricks were everywhere.

The Parrises were Puritans, like almost everyone in Salem Village. Puritans wore plain clothes and had strict customs. Their children were not allowed to dance or play music. The Puritans believed that children should be seen and not heard.

So it was surprising when on January 20 the minister's daughter, Betty, did something that Puritan children were not allowed to do.

She screamed.

The rest of the family rushed to see what was wrong. Had she fallen? Was there a wild animal in the house?

Betty did not seem hurt and she did not seem scared. Yet she answered everyone's questions with choking sounds and hoarse cries. This was strange.

On the following days she crawled into holes and squirmed under chairs, refusing to come out. Mr. Parris was puzzled. Nine-year-old Betty had never done anything like this before. She was sensitive and shy, but so were many children, and they did not go around screaming for no reason.

During the next week the minister's eleven-year-old niece, Abigail, began acting the same way. Now both girls were crying out and knocking over furniture. Soon eight older girls in the village were doing these things too. Some of them fell to the floor during meals. Others interrupted church services and public meetings with piercing shrieks and strange words.

The girls were not punished. Their parents did not think the girls did these things on purpose. But nobody knew who or what was responsible.

In early February, Mr. Parris asked the village doctor for help. The doctor examined Betty and the other girls carefully. He could not find anything wrong. He knew how to cure a sprained ankle—cover it with hot beer and honey. And he knew how to cure falling sickness—eat a powder made from frogs' livers ten times a day. But he did not know how to cure this strange madness. The doctor, however, had another explanation.

The girls were bewitched.

Mr. Parris agreed with the doctor. Like most Puritans, he believed in witches. They were often blamed for crop failure or unexplained illnesses. Perhaps witches were tormenting the girls.

This was a very serious matter, and it was the minister's duty to get to the bottom of it. So Mr. Parris told Betty and Abigail and the eight other girls to meet in his home. He also invited two ministers from nearby towns. Witchcraft was something that concerned them all.

The ten girls stood nervously before the three ministers. They were not used to talking to such important men. Important men had never paid this kind of attention to them before.

After everyone prayed for guidance, the room became quiet. The two visiting ministers were not sure if they believed the stories they were hearing. They stared at the girls, waiting to see what would happen.

Suddenly one girl groaned. Another gasped and fell like a stone. The other girls threw themselves around the room, knocking over chairs and crashing into the walls.

The two visiting ministers watched the girls closely. Their eyes widened. Their mouths fell open. No one could pretend to have such fits.

So the stories were true. In Salem Village witches were at work.

2

The First Arrests

The news passed quickly through Salem Village. The blacksmith heard it while he was repairing a sleigh runner. He told a farmer who had brought in his horse to be reshod. The farmer told his wife when he got home. And she shared the news with her friends at church on Sunday.

Salem Village was a small community of about five hundred people. Everyone there knew everyone else. To think that witches lived secretly among them was terrifying.

Almost everyone believed in witches. Witches had great powers given to them by the devil. Witches could cast spells and ride broomsticks through the air. They could make people fall in love and travelers lose their way in the woods. They could send out ghostly images of themselves too.

These ghostly images, or specters, were invisible to most people. The girls, it seemed, could see them. In the middle of their fits, they

cried out that specters were pinching and poking them. At one church meeting Abigail claimed to see a woman's specter sitting on a beam overhead, sucking on a yellow bird. Moments later the sheriff's daughter, Ann Putnam, cried out that a yellow bird was sitting on the minister's hat.

Such outbursts both frightened and fascinated people. They could not help being curious about the girls. And so far their curiosity had not gotten anyone into trouble. But that was about to change.

Until now the girls had named no one. But the ministers were stern with them. It was not enough to know that the girls were bewitched. They demanded to know who was bewitching them.

At first the girls would not talk.

Some of the villagers tried to help. If the girls would not name any witches on their own, perhaps they would take suggestions. One farmer mentioned a woman who had stared at his cow in the morning. That afternoon the cow had gotten sick. She must be a witch. Somebody else knew a woman who went out for walks after dark. Only a witch would do that.

The girls heard many stories like these, and still they named no one. But the pressure on them was mounting. If the girls could see specters, they should be able to identify them.

Finally, on February 29, the girls named three women—Sarah Good, Sarah Osburn, and the Parrises' slave Tituba. These three were immediately arrested.

The next day a large crowd gathered at the meeting house. The people who arrived early got seats inside. Others stood in the street.

Everyone had come to see the magistrates talk to the accused women. The magistrates were the town leaders. It was their job to decide if the women should be tried as witches in court.

Betty and the other girls were there as witnesses. They sat to one side, where they could see everything and where the magistrates could question them when necessary.

The three women were brought out one at a time. Sarah Good was a grumpy and unpopular person who sometimes went from door to door begging for food for her children. Sarah Osburn was an old, sickly woman. People gossiped about her because she had married

one of her servants. Tituba stood out among the Puritans because she had been born and raised on an island in the faraway Caribbean Sea.

When Sarah Good and Sarah Osburn were brought before the magistrates, the girls instantly fell to the ground. They twitched and twisted in pain. They screamed that the specters of both women were pinching and biting them.

The magistrates asked each woman if she could prove her innocence when the girls were so clearly suffering. Neither of them could, but they both claimed to be innocent anyway.

The magistrates were not swayed. They ordered the women held for trial in the nearby town of Salem.

The talk with Tituba went differently. Like the girls, she was not used to having important people listen to what she had to say. She seemed confused. At first she denied being a witch. But soon she confessed. She

said that she used magic. She added that she had seen a man and four women, including Sarah Good and Sarah Osburn, hurting the girls at different times. She even said she had once ridden on a broomstick with Sarah Good and Sarah Osburn behind her.

The magistrates considered Tituba as guilty as the others. But because she had confessed, her fate was different. As long as she was willing to help the magistrates find other witches, they would keep her in the Salem Village jail.

Now the magistrates were sure there were other witches. Their work had just begun.

3

Doubts and Secrets

As the days and weeks went by, the girls named many other men and women. The magistrates sent dozens of people to jail.

Not everyone agreed with the magistrates. A few people had doubts. They thought the girls should just be ignored. They said the girls were young and likely to imagine things.

Two women who felt this way soon found themselves accused of witchcraft. No wonder they say they doubt us, said the girls. They are witches themselves.

Before long the girls were accusing other doubters as well. The magistrates followed up every lead, and one by one these doubters were sent to jail to await their trials.

While the villagers were busy guessing who would be next, one of the girls, Mary Warren, made a surprising declaration. Not everything was as it seemed. Mary said that the other girls "did but dissemble."

In other words they were faking their fits.

Mary said no more, but she knew the real story. Before the witch hunt had started, she and the other girls had been meeting regularly with Tituba in Betty's house. They thought Tituba was very talented. She could read palms and tell fortunes. She knew strange and wonderful stories of life in the Caribbean.

The girls had greatly enjoyed such talk, especially in the winter when the cold, gray days seemed so dull. But they knew their parents would not approve. Telling fortunes

was not just a silly game to the Puritans. It was a sin.

The girls would have been punished for doing these things. Knowing this, they had kept the meetings a secret.

This secret must have been hard for Betty Parris to keep. She was the youngest. The pressure to tell may have built up inside her until it had found a way out. Perhaps that was why she screamed.

When the girls found out that Betty was acting strangely, they worried that she might tell their secret. They decided to take the attention away from Betty by imitating her. It was going to be like a game.

Of course, now it was more than a game. Some of the girls half believed their own stories about specters and witches. For them the line between truth and make-believe had already disappeared.

Mary Warren thought they had gone too far.

But the others were not about to stop. They were afraid that Mary would tell about the secret meetings. They had to deal with her before she said any more. So they accused her of joining with the devil. The devil did not like to see so many witches named, they said. Mary was trying to make the girls look bad so that no one would believe them. And if no

one believed them, the witches could go on making trouble.

Mary protested, but it did no good. She was brought before the magistrates too. When the magistrates questioned Mary, the other girls had fits. Mary was doing this to them, they cried out. Mary herself was not sure what to think. She fell into a fit and was taken away to jail.

The next day Mary changed her mind. She did not want to spend any more time in jail. Now she said that the girls were telling the truth.

The girls then agreed that Mary had not become a servant of the devil after all. She had broken away from him just in time.

Mary was soon released from jail. She never spoke about "dissembling" again. The girls felt better. Their secret was safe.

4

The Trials Begin

As spring came to Massachusetts, the snow melted and the birds returned. By May the muddy roads were dry and the trees were budding.

It was not a happy spring, though, for the almost one hundred people accused of witchcraft. They were all waiting for a trial and the chance to prove their innocence.

Puritans were brought to trial for many different offenses. Some were arrested for kissing in public. Others were fined for wearing the wrong kind of boots or falling asleep in church. More serious crimes resulted in whippings or long jail terms.

Witchcraft, like murder, was punishable by death. Three women had been hanged for practicing witchcraft in the seventy years since the Pilgrims had come to America. Dozens more in England had been hanged or burned at the stake.

The Salem trials began in late May and ran into the fall. Each day the seven judges sat solemnly in their chairs at the front of the courthouse. The jury of men sat to one side.

They were not the only ones in the Salem courthouse. The courtroom was filled with villagers. Farmers neglected their fields. Blacksmiths deserted their anvils. Cobblers left their shoes unsoled. The witchcraft trials were too exciting to miss.

Some of the accused witches were men, but most were women. All of the prisoners

looked weary. Some were very sick. The jails were dirty and crowded. Many of the prisoners had been locked up for weeks.

The accused were brought before the judges one by one. When a prisoner declared her innocence, the girls were called in. They were the star witnesses. Testifying against witches had become a kind of job for them. And they had become very good at it.

The accused person was a witch, they

declared again and again. Even now the prisoner's specter was attacking them. The girls showed that this was happening in many ways. They turned pale and then flushed. Their arms and legs stiffened and then suddenly relaxed. They described the specter so clearly that a few onlookers insisted they saw it too.

At Sarah Good's trial, one of the girls fell into a fit. She choked and gasped, as if she were wrestling with an invisible person. Then she seemed to faint.

When she awoke, she cried out that Sarah's specter had just tried to stab her with a knife. She had been lucky enough to break off the blade. She held up the blade for all to see.

The crowd in the courthouse was amazed.

But then a young man stepped forward. The blade belonged to him, he said. He had accidentally broken his knife earlier. The girl must have picked up the broken piece from the ground. He then showed the judges his knife handle, which indeed was missing most of the blade. The blade fit it exactly.

The judges were upset that the girl had invented this story. Do not lie to us, they told her sternly. But they still were not suspicious. They allowed her to continue testifying. They showed no concern that if she had lied once, she might lie again.

This trial and all the others were unfair. The prisoners had no good way to defend themselves, and nobody was really interested in what they had to say anyway. The judges and the jury had decided in advance that the accused witches were guilty.

No one spoke out about the unfair trials. The trials had become a spectator sport. A lot of the spectators were in no hurry to see them end.

5

The Madness Ends

During the long, hot summer eleven people were convicted of witchcraft and hanged. Several more died in prison while awaiting their trials. With the coming of fall, there were even more deaths as the witch hunt spread to other towns.

On September 22, eight condemned prisoners marched from the Salem jail up to Gallows Hill. People lined the streets, pushing and shouting. The constables escorting the prisoners warned the crowd to stay back.

It was their job to protect the prisoners so that they could go safely to their deaths.

The witch hunt was tearing towns apart. In Salem Village husbands testified against wives. Wives testified against husbands. Children condemned their own parents. Lifelong friends betrayed one another. In the town of Andover over forty people were arrested after the Salem authorities sent two of the girls to help identify witches. Several Andover witnesses even claimed a dog was a witch. The authorities had it killed.

People besides the girls were now claiming to see specters too. For anyone with a grudge against somebody, the best way to get even was to accuse that person of witchcraft. There were a lot of grudges in Massachusetts. At the rate things were going, the witches would soon outnumber everyone else.

Altogether over two hundred people had been arrested. The girls, the judges, and the others caught up in the witch hunt thought there would be more.

But they were wrong.

Public sentiment was changing. People said the witch hunt must end. There had been too many deaths. Too many respectable citizens had been condemned.

Ministers were also speaking out against the trials. They believed that the girls did see specters, but they were not sure they should believe what the specters said. Specters were clearly the work of the devil. Since the devil could not be trusted, why should his specters

be trusted either? What if the specters took the form of innocent people to fool the girls? Spectral evidence alone, they said, should not be enough to convict a witch. "It were better that ten suspected witches should escape," said one minister, "than that one innocent Person should be condemned."

The governor listened to the ministers and other advisers who thought the witch madness had gone too far. In mid-October he stated that no further imprisonments were to be made on the charge of witchcraft. Two weeks later he dismissed the witchcraft court.

The Massachusetts legislature then created a higher court to try the remaining witchcraft cases. By now spectral evidence was no longer allowed. Without the girls and without the specters, only three persons accused of witchcraft were found guilty. The governor, however, reprieved their death sentences, and they were set free.

At the end of May 1693 the governor pardoned anyone still imprisoned on witchcraft charges. It was too late for the nineteen people who had been hanged and for those others who had died in prison. But for the rest their ordeal was over at last.

6

What Happened Afterward

After the Salem witch trials ended, the Massachusetts legislature voted to pay the families of the deceased for their losses. The amount of money they were offered was small, and in any event it was no comfort to the people of Salem Village. Money could not bring back the dead.

There was no happy ending for Mr. Parris, either. Once the danger was past, Tituba took back her story of being a witch. Now she said the minister had beaten her and made her

confess. This angered some members of the church. They spoke out against Mr. Parris for his part in the witchcraft madness. Their anger did not go away. In 1696 Parris's wife, Elizabeth, died, and the next year he quit his post and left Salem Village forever.

The girls themselves were never punished. They simply went back to the ordinary lives they had led before. In time, Betty Parris and some of the other girls got married and had families. No one ever asked the girls to explain their strange fits and visions, and only one girl ever offered to do this. But she was twenty-six years old when she finally spoke up.

In 1706 Ann Putnam stood in church to make a confession. The years since the witch-craft trials had been hard for Ann. Her parents had died, and she had raised her young brothers and sisters by herself.

Now she apologized for her acts fourteen years earlier. None of the things she had said then were true, she told everyone. There were no witches or specters. She had not made them up on purpose, though. The devil had

tricked her. She begged forgiveness from God and from all those whom she had harmed.

The lesson she had learned was an important one. Ann Putnam, Betty Parris, Abigail Williams, Mary Warren, and the other girls did not set out to destroy people's lives. But they started something that quickly grew too big for them to handle. Their small, guilty secret ended up causing the deaths of innocent people.

They were not the only guilty ones, though. The judges, the ministers, and the neighbors who testified against each other also shared in the blame. These people were too eager to find evil where it did not exist. The Salem witch hunt was a time when fear and hate ruled over common sense.